CHIMPANZEES

A TRUE BOOK

by

Patricia A. Fink Martin

Children's Press®
A Division of Grolier Publishing

New York London Hong Kong Sydney
Danbury, Connecticut

Chimpanzees like to clown around and make funny faces.

Reading Consultant
Linda Cornwell
*Coordinator of School Quality
and Professional Improvement
Indiana State Teachers Association*

Content Consultant
Kathy Carlstead, Ph.D.
*National Zoological Park
Washington, D.C.*

The photograph on the cover shows a chimpanzee making a tool. The photograph on the title page shows a chimpanzee eating termites off a plant stem.

**Visit Children's Press® on the Internet at:
http://publishing.grolier.com**

Library of Congress Cataloging-in-Publication Data

Martin, Patricia A. Fink, 1955–
    Chimpanzee / by Patricia A. Fink Martin.
        p. cm. — (A true book)
    Includes bibliographical references and index.
    Summary: Describes the behavior, habitat, life cycle, and physical
characteristics of this much-studied ape.
    ISBN: 0-516-21572-8 (lib. bdg.)   0-516-27013-3 (pbk.)
    1. Chimpanzee—Juvenile literature. [1. Chimpanzee .] I. Title.
II. Series.
QL737.P96M37   2000
599.885—dc21
                                                                99-17068
                                                                CIP
                                                                AC

Contents

Do you see like a hawk (left), swim like a fish (middle), or run like a deer (bottom)?

Our Closest Living Relative

Has anyone ever told you that you have eyes like a hawk? Or that you eat like a bird? Are you as strong as an ox? Do you swim like a fish or run like a deer?

Of course, these are just common sayings. You are really not like any of those animals. The animal that looks and acts most like us lives in the forests of east, west, and central Africa.

Its body is shaped a lot like ours, but it is covered with dark hair. Only its face, hands, and ears are bare. Its arms hang down below its knees, and its legs are short. Can you guess which animal it is? It is the chimpanzee!

Chimpanzees belong to a group of animals called the

Chimpanzees are a lot like us.

Like the chimpanzee, the gorilla (left) and the orangutan (right) are great apes.

great apes. Great apes are larger than monkeys and have no tail. Orangutans, bonobos, and gorillas are also great apes. Scientists place monkeys, apes, and humans into a group of mammals called primates.

Primates are smart animals. They have large brains and hands made for grasping. They can use their fingers to pick up and hold objects. Most primates have eyes that face forward, so they can tell whether the objects they see are nearby or far away.

Moving from Place to Place

Have you ever played on a jungle gym or monkey bars? When you swing from rung to rung on a jungle gym, you move like a chimpanzee. When a chimp grabs a branch overhead, powerful muscles help the animal hang by one

Chimpanzees can grab onto tree branches and swing through the trees.

hand. Quickly, the ape swings from one branch to the next.

The body of a chimpanzee is designed for spending time in trees. Its long hands can easily wrap around tree branches. Its feet are built for

A chimp's feet work just like its hands.

climbing. A large space separates its big toe from the other toes. The big toe acts like a thumb, so the chimpanzee's feet work just like hands. They can grab a tree trunk and hold on tight.

A chimpanzee can travel on the ground too. When it walks on all fours, only the soles of its feet and its knuckles touch the ground. Special pads protect its hands from the rough forest floor.

A chimpanzee walks on all fours when it travels across the ground.

What Is for Dinner?

Chimpanzees roam the forest all day in search of food. They eat fruits, young leaves, flowers, nuts, and seeds. They also eat insects, such as termites and ants, and other animals.

Some of the foods that chimps like are hard to get to.

This chimpanzee is eating a fig.

Termites are hard to reach inside their dirt mounds. Nuts are hard to crack. But chimps are smart enough to use tools. They strip leaves from stems, and use the stems to

This chimpanzee is using the stem of a plant to "fish" for termites.

pull termites out of their mound. They use rocks to crack open nuts.

Chimpanzees are closely related to humans, but for many years scientists thought our diets were very different. Then, in 1975, a scientist named Jane Goodall saw a chimpanzee eating meat. Since then she has seen male chimps hunt and kill other mammals. They hunt alone or in small groups for monkeys, small antelopes, and other medium-size animals.

Jane Goodall spent many years studying chimpanzees in East Africa.

Clever Chimps

Chimpanzees are very good at using tools. When a chimp sticks a plant stem into a termite mound, the insects bite the stem. Then the chimp pulls the stem out of the mound with termites still hanging on by their jaws! Quickly the chimpanzee pops the insects into its mouth. Termites make a juicy, crunchy meal. After eating fruit, chimpanzees use leaves to wipe their sticky hands. They also use leaves to scoop up water from places they cannot reach with their mouths.

Chimpanzees are skilled at using tools.
This one is using a stick to catch termites
living in a log.

This chimpanzee family group belongs to a larger community.

Chimp Society

Every chimpanzee belongs to a large group, or community. A community may have up to 100 chimps. All the chimpanzees in a community know one another. Each one has a certain rank, or position. The highest-ranking member is a male called the alpha male.

When an alpha male feels threatened, it tries to scare away its enemy.

Sometimes the alpha male puts on a show—with lots of action and noise! He is reminding everyone that he is the boss. His hair rises up. He breaks off a tree branch and shakes it wildly in the air.

Then he tosses the branch aside and jumps into a tree. Suddenly the whole tree begins to shake. The alpha male screams, leaps to the ground, and then charges through the trees. The other chimps run in all directions.

When an alpha male screams, the other chimps run in all directions.

Male chimpanzees fight often. Sometimes it is only for show, but sometimes they hurt each other. After a fight, the chimpanzees always make up. One chimp hugs the

After a fight, chimpanzees often hug. Touching helps them feel calm and safe.

Chimpanzees often groom one another.

other or touches his hand or head. The chimps stroke each other's fur and pick out dirt, seeds, and insects. This is called grooming.

Babies are special members of chimp society. All the chimps in a community want to see and touch a new baby. But the mother guards her young carefully.

A mother chimpanzee watches her baby closely and protects it from harm.

This mother chimp is ready to catch her baby if it falls.

A mother chimp usually cares for her baby alone. She may have some help from an older child, but fathers are not part of the family.

When a chimp is very young, its mother holds it close.

For the first few months, the mother chimp holds her baby close. She feeds it with milk from her breasts. When the mother travels, the baby rides under her belly. When the young chimp is a little older, it rides on its mother's back.

By the time a chimp is 5 months old, it eats some fruits and leaves. Most young chimps drink mother's milk until they are 5 years old. Then the chimp starts growing up. Most chimps become adults when they are between 11 and 15 years old.

A group of chimps wakes up in Gombe
Stream National Park in Tanzania.

 A Chimp's Day

A chimp's day begins and ends in the trees. Early in the morning, the leaves rustle high in the treetops. A chimp is climbing to the ground. Soon, another chimp leaves its treetop bed.

The two chimpanzees wander off to look for food. They

When a chimp finds a good source of food, it calls out to other chimps. All the chimps share the feast.

hear loud hoots and run toward the sound. A huge fig tree has produced its fruit.

Almost a dozen apes are already sucking the sweet, sticky figs.

The chimps climb the tree, hooting with excitement. They greet the others by touching their hands and heads. Soon the apes settle down and eat the delicious fruit.

Chimps usually rest at mid-day. Mother chimps groom their babies. Several males sit in a group and groom one another. The youngsters play. Later, the chimps search for more food.

Late in the evening, each chimp makes a nest for itself. Only mother chimps share their beds. It takes just 5 minutes to make a comfortable bed. First, they twist and bend leafy twigs. Then they grab a few leaves from branches above their heads. High above the ground, the chimps rest for the night.

What Is a Bonobo?

Have you ever heard of a bonobo? How about a pygmy chimp? Both these names are used to describe an animal that looks a lot like a chimp. In fact, for many years people thought bonobos were chimps. But now we know they are another kind of great ape.

A bonobo looks a lot like a chimpanzee.

Bonobos are chimpanzee look-alikes. But if you look closely, you will notice some differences. Bonobos have thinner bodies with long arms

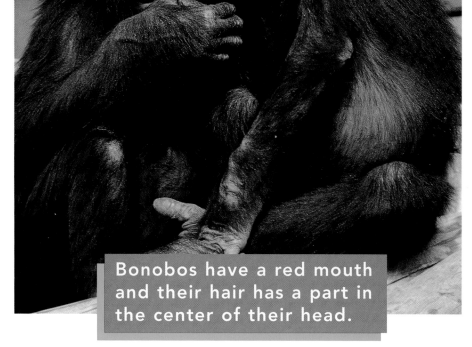

Bonobos have a red mouth and their hair has a part in the center of their head.

and legs. Their skin is dark, but their mouth is red. The hair on their head always seems to be parted in the middle!

A 2-year-old bonobo grooms its mother.

But it is not just the way they look that makes bonobos different from chimpanzees. They act differently too. Bonobos spend more time in the trees. They weigh less than chimpanzees, so they can climb much higher in search of food. Sometimes bonobos even jump from tree to tree!

Like chimps, bonobos are social animals—they like the company of other bonobos. But in a bonobo community, females form close friend-ships with other females. They groom and touch each other often.

Chimpanzees are endangered species.
Will they be able to survive?

Endangered Animals

In the wild, the chimpanzee and the bonobo are both endangered species. Poachers hunt them, and the forests they live in are being destroyed. In some African countries, the chimp has been completely wiped out. No one knows for certain how many bonobos are left.

People all over the world are trying to help the great apes. You can help too. Join a group that protects these animals. Tell your friends about them. Start a class project to raise money to support chimps whose parents have been killed. These great apes are part of the primate family. Chimpanzees are our closest living relatives.

Scientists hope to learn as much as they can about chimpanzees. The more we know, the better our chances of saving them.

To Find Out More

Here is a list of more materials on chimpanzees and bonobos. Use these resources to learn more about our closest living relatives!

Books and Videos

Books

Elwood, Ann, **Chimpanzees and Bonobos.** Zoobook Series, Wildlife Education, Ltd., 1990.

Fromer, Julie. **Jane Goodall: Living with the Chimps.** Twenty-first Century Books, 1992.

Goodall, Jane. **The Chimpanzee Family Book.** Picture Book Studio, 1989.

———. **Jane Goodall's Animal World: Chimps.** Macmillan Publishing Company, 1989.

———. **My Life with the Chimpanzees.** A Minstral Book, 1988.

Powzyk, Joyce. **Tracking Wild Chimpanzees.** Lothrop, Lee, & Shepard Books, 1988.

Videos

Among the Wild Chimpanzees. National Geographic Society, 1984.

The Life and Legend of Jane Goodall. National Geographic Society, 1990.

The New Chimpanzee. National Geographic Society, 1995.

Organizations and Online Sites

The Bonobo
*http://www.oit.itd.umich.
edu/bio/doc.cgi/Chorda-
ta/Mammalia/Primates/
Hominidae/Pan_paniscus.ftl*

This site will tell you what
bonobos look like, where
they live, what they eat,
and more.

The Bonobo Protection Fund
Georgia State University
Georgia State University
Plaza
3401 Panthersville Rd.
Atlanta, GA 30303
*http://www.gsu.edu/
~wwwbpf/bpf/*

Don't Call Me Monkey
*http://www.tcfhe.com/
Dunston/Not/Content/
dontCallMe/index.html*

Not all primates are mon-
keys. This site will teach
you the difference between
monkeys, prosimians, and
great apes.

The Jane Goodall Institute
P.O. Box 14890
Silver Spring, MD 20911
*http://www.gsn.org/
project.jgi/index.html*

International Primate Protection League
P.O. Box 766
Summerville, SC 29484
http://www.ippl.org

World Wildlife Fund
1250 24th Street, NW
Washington, DC 20037
http://www.wwf.org/

Important Words

alpha male the top male in certain animal communities

ape a large, tailless primate

endangered species a living thing in danger of dying out

great ape the largest of the apes, the group includes the orangutan, the gorilla, the chimpanzee, and the bonobo

groom to pick an animal's fur clean of dirt, insects, and dead skin

poacher a person who hunts and kills animals when it is against the law

primate a mammal with hands that grasp, and a large brain

Index

Meet the Author

Patricia A. Fink Martin has a doctorate in biology. After working in the laboratory and teaching for 10 years, she began writing science books for children. *Booklist* chose her first book, *Animals that Walk on Water*, as one of the ten best animal books for children in 1998. Dr. Martin lives in Tennessee with her husband, Jerry, and their daughter, Leslie.

Photographs ©: Aaron Norman: 4 center; Animals Animals: 38 (M. Colbeck), 11 (Zig Leszczynski); ENP Images: 8 left (Michael Durham), 1, 4 top, 7, 8 right, 12, 15, 16, 20, 30, 40 (Gerry Ellis); National Geographic Image Collection: 32 (Michael K. Nichols), 17; Photo Researchers: cover, 2, 13, 22, 36 (Tim Davis), 23, 26 (Nigel J. Dennis), 4 bottom (S. J. Krasemann), 43 (Susan Kuklin), 19, 24 (Renee Lynn), 25, 27, 28 (Tom McHugh), 37 (R. Van Nostrand).